Learning Patterns

Pattern Language 3.0 Catalogue Series

Learning Patterns: A Pattern Language for Creative Learning

Presentation Patterns: A Pattern Language for Creative Presentation

Collaboration Patterns: A Pattern Language for Creative Collaborations

Words for a Journey: The Art of Being with Dementia

Survival Language: A Pattern Language for Surviving Earthquakes

Change Making Patterns: A Pattern Language for Fostering Social Entrepreneurship

Meta-Pattern Language Catalogue Series

Pattern Illustrating Patterns: A Pattern Language for Pattern Illustrating

Learning Patterns
A Pattern Language for Creative Learning

Takashi Iba
with Iba Laboratory

 **CreativeShift**

Copyright © 2014 by Takashi Iba.

All rights reserved. This book or any portion thereof may not be reproduced or used in any manner whatsoever without the express written permission of the publisher except for the use of brief quotations in a book review or scholarly journal.

The authors and publisher have taken care in the preparation of this book, but no liability is assumed for incidental or consequential damages in connection with or arising out of the use of the information contained herein.

First Printing: 2014
V.1.01 (2018)

ISBN 978-1-312-40885-2

CreativeShift, Inc.
SA Bldg., 3F, Yoshidacho 112-2, Totsuka,
Yokohama, Kanagawa, Japan zip 244-0817
E-mail: contact@ml.creativeshift.co.jp

Learning Patterns Project, Iba Laboratory, Keio University
Takashi Iba, Toko Miyake, Kazeto Shimonishi,
Tsuyoshi Kato, Yuji Kobayashi, Natsumi Yotsumoto
Mariko Hanabusa, Mayu Iida, Mami Sakamoto
Special thanks to Taichi Isaku

Illustrations by Toko Miyake & Takashi Iba.

*For everyone who wants to live more creative
and helps others live more creative.*

Contents

Acknowledgements	xi
Preface	1

Introduction   3

Learning Patterns	5
How to read Learning Patterns	7
The Philosophy of Pattern Languages	9

The Patterns   11

The Core Patterns   13
- Creative Learning — 14
- Opportunity for Learning — 16
- Learning by Creating — 18
- Open Learning — 20

Patterns for Opportunity   23
- Jump In — 24
- Copycat Learner — 26

Effective Asking	28
Output-Driven Learning	30
Daily Use of Foreign Language	32
Playful Learning	34
Tornado of Learning	36
Chain of Excitement	38
Quantity brings Quality	40
Skill Embodiment	42
Language Shower	44
Tangible Growth	46

Patterns for Creation — 49

Thinking in Action	50
Prototyping	52
Field Diving	54
A Bug's-Eye & Bird's-Eye View	56
Hidden Connections	58
Triangular Dig	60
Passion for Exploration	62
Brain Switch	64
Fruit Farming	66
Attractive Expressions	68
The First-Draft-Halfway-Point	70
Acceleration to the Next	72

Patterns for Openness — 75

Community of Learning	76
Serendipitous Encounters	78
Good Rivals	80
Talking Thinker	82
Learning by Teaching	84
Firm Determination	86

Questioning Mind	88
The Right Way	90
Brave Changes	92
Frontier Finder	94
Self-Producer	96
Be Extreme!	98

How To Use 101

How To Use Learning Patterns 103

Learning Pattern Cards 107

Pattern Dialogue Workshop 109

Creation Process of Learning Patterns 111

References 115

Acknowledgements

We would like to thank to Richard Gabriel, Linda Rising, Joseph Yoder, Rebecca Wirfs-Brock, Jenny Quillien, Lise Hvatum, Bob Hanmer, Mary Lynn Manns, Christian Kohls, and Christian Köppe for encouraging our quest to create a new type of pattern language. We also want to thank our shepherds Pam Rostal, Yuji Yamano, and Pam Rostal, and also workshop participants for giving kind comments for some patterns in Learning Patterns at the PLoP2009, AsianPLoP2010, and PLoP2011 conferences. Additionally, my greatest honor goes to all members of related projects, such as the Presentation Patterns Project and the Collaboration Patterns Project, for their valuable work.

Preface

In the recent complex society, identifying problems and creatively thinking of solutions from various perspectives is essential. People need to learn by constructing their own living knowledge based on their situation and not by merely memorizing existing ideas; Learning how to generate new ideas and how to think is also necessary; that is, a *Creative Learning*.

In *Creative Learning*, learner creates opportunities for learning by himself/herself by launching and implementing his/her own project, and learn through actively creating with others. How can such *Creative Learning* be achieved? Secrets to *Creative Learning* are scribed in this book.

Learning Patterns in this book presents 40 distinct patterns that show tips, methods, and views for a Creative Learning. The focus is on problem finding and problem solving in various learning situations.

This book is intended to support you in various ways. First, it helps you reflect on your learning methods. Second, it provides opportunities for you to know new, better ways to learn. Third, it encourages you to discuss about your own ways of learning with your friends, colleagues, and mentors.

Read through the pages and use any or all the Learning Patterns to make your learning more creative!

Introduction

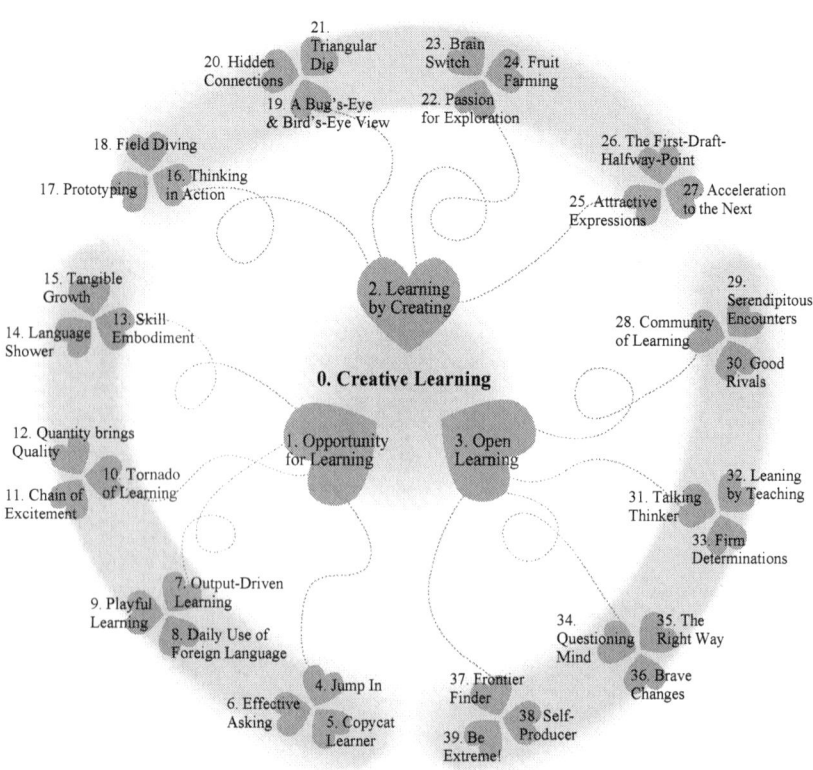

Learning Patterns

In *Creative Learning*, learner creates opportunities for learning by himself/herself by launching and implementing his/her own project, and learn through actively creating with others. The Learning Patterns strives to verbalize tips on achieving such learning.

The Learning Patterns consists of 40 patterns. At the center of the pattern language is pattern No.0: *Creative Learning*, and the three main patterns for such learning: *Opportunity for Learning* (1), *Learning by Creating* (2), and *Open Learning* (3) surround the *Creative Learning*.

The subsequent patterns are grouped into three categories. The first group, patterns Nos. 4 – 15, relates to *Opportunity for Learning* (1). The second group of patterns, Nos.16 – 27 shows patterns related to *Learning by Creating* (2). The third group, pattern Nos.28 – No.39 relates to *Open Learning* (3). These patterns help learner achieve a *Creative Learning* through their interactions.

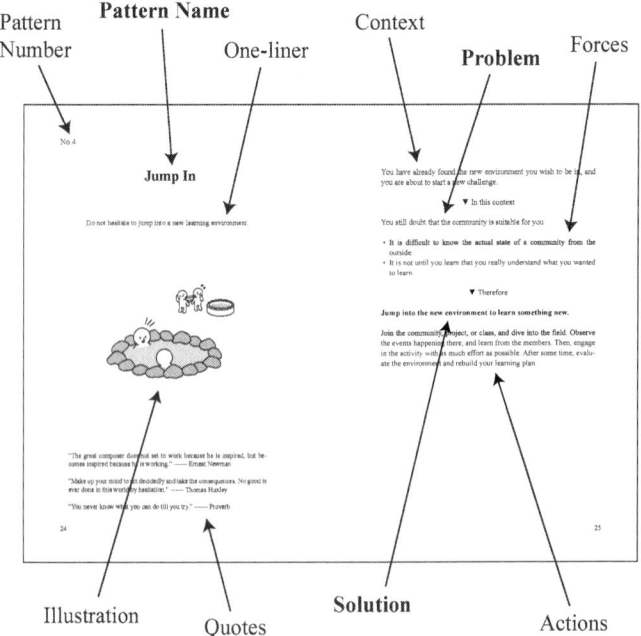

How to read Learning Patterns

The patterns in this book are written in the same format. On the top left side of the page, you will see the Pattern Number, Pattern Name, One-liners to explain the pattern, and Illustration. At the bottom of the page are Quotes related to the pattern.

The left hand page gives you a brief idea of the pattern's meaning. The Pattern Name, for example, gives the pattern a short memorable name for easy reference that accurately describes the pattern. The One-liner, Illustration, and Quotes assist you in understanding a living image of the pattern.

The right hand page offers more detail about the pattern. Listing from the top, the Context, Problem, Forces, Solution, and Actions are all described.

The right page starts out by describing the Context in which the pattern should be used. Followed by the words "In this context," a Problem that is likely to occur under the context is written. The Forces, which are bulleted below this, are unavoidable laws about the aspects of human nature that make the Problem difficult to overcome.

Followed by a "Therefore," the Solution to the Problem is highlighted in bold. Finally, the Actions explain the rather abstract Solution and give you some concrete actions.

The Philosophy of Pattern Languages

The Learning Patterns are based on the philosophy of Pattern Languages, which was first proposed by architect Christopher Alexander. A pattern language is the lingua franca for architectural design and it provides a method that allows everyone to become involved in the design process. Alexander found that certain architectural rules repeatedly appeared in the design of towns and buildings. He called these rules "patterns," and proposed a way of developing them as a language.

More generally, a pattern language obtains the design knowledge arising from a person's experience and summarizes it in the form of a pattern. It pairs a problem occurring in a certain context of design with its solution and gives it a name. A pattern language's users must determine which pattern to use on the basis of both context and fit with the abstract solution to their specific situation.

There are two basic reasons for writing and sharing a pattern language. First, by clearly expressing the knowledge gained from experience, a written pattern gives tools to those with less experienced to solve problems in a more sophisticated manner. Second, pattern languages offer a common vocabulary, allowing reference to the complex relationships existing between each component, which are otherwise often difficult to verbalize.

This idea of pattern languages was soon introduced and applied to the design process within other professional areas, such as software design, organizational design, and educational design. As its usefulness has been proven since its first appearance, the pattern language approach is expected to be continually applied to many other professional areas.

As mentioned above, the original idea of pattern languages to transcribe practical design knowledge was proposed by architect Christopher Alexander in the late 1970s. Ten years later, Alexander's idea of pattern languages was adopted in the field of software design.

Since the late 1990s, pattern languages have begun to be applied to an increasing range of fields to encompass creative human actions such as education, organizational change, learning, presentation, collaboration, social innovation, disaster prevention, life design, and even beauty in daily life. To distinguish this new generation of pattern languages that describe patterns for creative human actions, we have named them "Pattern Language 3.0."

The Learning Patterns introduced here is a pattern language, more strictly a pattern language 3.0, that helps learner achieve *Creative Learning*. Along with discovering methods to engage in effective learning, we hope you can also imagine the possibilities that pattern languages offer.

The Patterns

The Core Patterns

Nos.0 - 3

0   Creative Learning

1   Opportunity for Learning
2   Learning by Creating
3   Open Learning

No.0

Creative Learning

Make your learning more creative.

"It is not knowledge, but the means of gaining knowledge which I have to teach." —— Thomas Arnold

"A creative process creates the object of the creation, but also simultaneously gives the creators a chance to evolve and grow out of their current selves. In other words not only the creation, but also the creator must be created for a process to be truly creative. The more creative the process is the more the creator has to gain and grow from it." —— Jiro Kawakita

In a complex and fluid society, it is essential to identify problems and think of solutions from various perspectives and with a creative mind.

▼ In this context

Opportunities for improving your creative skills and knowledge are limited.

- There are several ways of learning.
- The opportunities provided are not always suitable to your needs.
- To improve your creative skills, it is necessary to learn by constructing living knowledge based on your creative experience, not just by memorizing existing ideas.

▼ Therefore

Create opportunities for learning by yourself by launching and implementing your own project, and learn through actively creating with others.

Create your own *Opportunity for Learning* (1) based on your interests, without waiting for someone to provide you with an opportunity. To make this happen, launch your own project, and conduct *Learning by Creating* (2) as part of the project. Along the way, share your learning process and collaborate with others to deepen each other's learning as *Open Learning* (3).

No.1

Opportunity for Learning

Opportunities for learning are created,
not chanced upon or waited for.

"A wise man will make more opportunities than he finds." —— Francis Bacon

"In the fields of observation chance favors only the prepared mind." —— Louis Pasteur

"Action is the foundational key to all success." —— Pablo Picasso

You are ready to learn, and perhaps you have a few expectations.

▼ In this context

There are few good opportunities for learning compared to your expectations.

- The opportunities provided are not always suitable for you.
- It is not easy to notice what is not there.

▼ Therefore

Create your own opportunities for learning based on your interests.

Consider your interests, and specify the knowledge and skills you want to learn. Then, seek information related to your needs, and understand how to learn. If you find, immerse yourself in the environment to start learning.

No.2

Learning by Creating

Learn through actively creating,
rather than through memorization.

"Acquiring is always secondary, and instrumental to the act of inquiring."
— John Dewey

"The true delight is in the finding out rather than in the knowing."
— Isaac Asimov

"All the world is a laboratory to the inquiring mind." — Martin H. Fischer

You have started to learn, and maybe you want more excitement.

▼ In this context

You are not willing to learn just by acquiring knowledge and skills.

- It is difficult to work on what you are not interested in.
- The necessity of achieving the goal enhances your motivation for learning.
- Practice often teaches you what you have not known.
- Acquired knowledge is improved by practice.

▼ Therefore

Launch and implement your own project to improve your knowledge and skills.

First, grasp up-to-date knowledge and think about what you need. Then, improve your knowledge and skills by creating projects and through fieldwork to make new discoveries. Finally, reflect on what you have learned, and think about a better way to deepen understanding. See also *Collaboration Patterns*, another volume of this catalogue series, about patterns to achieve Creative Collaborations.

No.3

Open Learning

Open your learning process to others and your future.

"Dialogue is really aimed at going into the whole thought process and changing the way the thought process occurs collectively." —— David Bohm

You have already learned to some extent, and you want to deepen your learning.

▼ In this context

Learning tends to be closed. It is difficult to deepen understanding on your own.

- A person has limited knowledge.
- It is difficult to notice your lack of understanding.
- There is little opportunity to meet people who share similar interests as you.

▼ Therefore

Share your learning process and collaborate with others to deepen each other's learning.

Make friends or rivals who will work with you, and share your current results and get feedback before you finish your project. After collaborating with others, persevere with utmost effort.

Patterns for Opportunity

Nos.4 - 15

4	Jump In
5	Copycat Learner
6	Effective Asking
7	Output-Driven Learning
8	Daily Use of Foreign Language
9	Playful Learning
10	Tornado of Learning
11	Chain of Excitement
12	Quantity brings Quality
13	Skill Embodiment
14	Language Shower
15	Tangible Growth

No.4

Jump In

Do not hesitate to jump into a new learning environment.

"The great composer does not set to work because he is inspired, but becomes inspired because he is working." —— Ernest Newman

"Make up your mind to act decidedly and take the consequences. No good is ever done in this world by hesitation." —— Thomas Huxley

"You never know what you can do till you try." —— Proverb

You have already found the new environment you wish to be in, and you are about to start a new challenge.

▼ In this context

You still doubt that the community is suitable for you.

- It is difficult to know the actual state of a community from the outside.
- It is not until you learn that you really understand what you wanted to learn.

▼ Therefore

Jump into the new environment to learn something new.

Join the community, project, or class, and dive into the field. Observe the events happening there, and learn from the members. Then, engage in the activity with as much effort as possible. After some time, evaluate the environment and rebuild your learning plan.

No.5

Copycat Learner

Begin by imitating the master.

"Those who do not want to imitate anything, produce nothing."
—— Salvador Dali

"Bad artists copy. Good artists steal." —— Pablo Picasso

"The greatest education in the world is watching the masters at work."
—— Michael Jackson

You have just started to learn new skills, maybe after performing *Jump In* (4).

▼ In this context

It is difficult to find your own way from the beginning.

- It takes a long time to acquire skills.
- Uniqueness or originality is recognized only by comparison.

▼ Therefore

Begin by imitating others to learn.

Find a role model to respect as a master. It doesn't matter whether you are in the same field. Observe their ways of thinking, acting, and communicating, and keep practicing as they do. Perform *Effective Asking* (6), if necessary. Thereafter, adopt their ways as your own.

No.6

Effective Asking

The right questions will bring about
great improvements.

"Asking the right questions takes as much skill as giving the right answers."
—— Robert Half

"The thankful receiver bears a plentiful harvest." —— William Blake

You got stuck, and you cannot figure out the way to go forward by yourself.

▼ In this context

It is difficult to get the right answers when you ask vague questions.

- Awareness of lack of abilities is the starting point for acquiring ability.
- Ability cannot be enhanced without practice.

▼ Therefore

Clarify where you got stuck, and then seek advice.

Write down what you have achieved so far and what you want to do next. Look for persons who can advice you on your problems. If necessary, ask someone or search on the Web. Take notes of the advice you received, and take action by yourself based on the advice. Make notes open to the public for other learners, which is good for your community and your own learning.

No.7

Output-Driven Learning

Creating outputs teaches you
what the input needs to be.

"I am always doing that which I cannot do, in order that I may learn how to do it." —— Pablo Picasso

"Necessity is the mother of taking chances." —— Mark Twain

"Once we accept our limits, we go beyond them." —— Albert Einstein

You are working on acquiring new knowledge and skills.

▼ In this context

It is difficult to keep learning if the necessity is unclear.

- Creation and practice make you aware of your limitations.
- Necessity is the mother of learning.
- It is difficult to work hard for things that are weakly related to you.

▼ Therefore

Create output to acquire knowledge and improve your skills.

Involve yourself in the situation of creating something as an output, and recognize what you cannot do. Then, acquire new knowledge and skills to overcome these difficulties. Evaluate your output from various standpoints and the feedback of others, and consider what needs to be improved in the near future.

No.8

Daily Use of Foreign Language

Use a foreign language daily,
using aspects related to your life and interests.

"Words are tied to reality when their meanings depend ... on a speaker's commitments about the truth. But there is a way in which words are tied to reality even more directly. They are not just about facts about the word stored in a person's head but are woven into the causal fabric of the world itself." —— Steven Pinker

You've recognized that you need to read, write, and speak a foreign language in the near future.

▼ In this context

It is difficult to read, write, and speak a foreign language without any practice.

- A person's time is limited.
- A person's knowledge is limited.
- It takes time to master a language.
- Difficulty conveying your idea depends on your stocks of expressions in a particular language.

▼ Therefore

Engage yourself in reading, writing, and speaking a foreign language in your daily life.

Establish an environment in which to use a foreign language. For example, a blog or a diary, or create opportunities to speak in a foreign language. Pick your topic. Content should focus on a particular topic. For example, the content might explain your interests or describe your daily life. First, write a few sentences on your topic. Then, search for books, papers, and webpages in the foreign language and learn the vocabulary and expressions used in them. It is good to find a friend or colleague who is writing about similar topics and read each other's essays. The presence of readers — be it *Community of Learning* (28) or *Good Rivals* (30) — is always a strong motivation for a writer.

No.9

Playful Learning

It is easier to learn something new
if you take pleasure in the results.

"Put your hand on a hot stove for a minute, and it seems like an hour. Sit with a pretty girl for an hour, and it seems like a minute. THAT'S relativity."
—— Albert Einstein

The process of learning bores you.

▼ In this context

Learning as a duty is ineffective and painful.

- It is difficult to continue tedious work.
- It is difficult to maintain motivation for ineffective learning.
- Necessity is the mother of learning.

▼ Therefore

Add "play" to your learning process.

Associate what you learn with your interests. When you want to learn the methods of data analysis, analyze the data you are interested in and you will enjoy learning the skills. When you want to learn the techniques of programming, start by programming a game if you like playing video games.

No.10

Tornado of Learning

Learn powerfully like the vacuum of a tornado,
involving knowledge that you need.

"Information is not knowledge." —— Albert Einstein

You've found there are many resources, for example, books, articles, and courses on your interests.

▼ In this context

Effective learning is not brought about by passively receiving information.

- It tends to be boring to read or listen to one-way information.
- Since lectures and books don't provide the most suitable knowledge for each learner, you have to seek connections within the realm of your own interests.
- It is necessary to relate to new things with the knowledge you have already acquired to understand them.

▼ Therefore

Collect information related to your interests, like the vacuum of a tornado.

Think about what your interests are. This will be the origin of the "tornado" of learning. Choose classes or books and compare them to your own interests. You do not have to choose only one interest. Be aggressive about grabbing what you want to know. When you take notes and read books, focus on what you think is important. Do not just store the given knowledge. Mix it up and find connections between the knowledge. Write your ideas in notebooks when you are reading.

No.11

Chain of Excitement

Excitement comes to people who crave for it.

"Wonder is the desire of knowledge." —— Thomas Aquinas

"The scientist does not study nature because it is useful; he studies it because he delights in it, and he delights in it because it is beautiful."
—— Henri Poincaré

"We keep moving forward, opening new doors, and doing new things, because we're curious and curiosity keeps leading us down new paths."
—— Walt Disney

You have made some learning progress, and perhaps you think you've almost achieved your initial goal.

▼ In this context

It is not easy to actively continue exploring and studying.

- It is difficult to continue working intensely on tedious tasks.
- It is easy to be impressed not only by the beauty of arts and nature but also by intellectual excitement.
- Intellectual excitement and academic experiences motivate you to study.

▼ Therefore

Feel the strong emotion of accomplishment, which will motivate your learning.

Make the connection between newly acquired knowledge and already known knowledge to compare the differences. Moreover, always look at how your perceptions of the world change when you grasp new knowledge. Focus on your emotion when new discoveries and experiences impress you.

No.12

Quantity brings Quality

Viewing a subject from different angles is necessary
for a deeper understanding.

"Learning is finding out what you already know." —— Richard Bach

"The real voyage of discovery consists not in seeking new landscapes but in having new eyes." —— Marcel Proust

"Mindsets play strange tricks on us. We see things the way our minds have instructed our eyes to see" —— Muhammad Yunus

You are realizing that you have only a shallow understanding of what you are interested in.

▼ In this context

It is difficult to deepen your understanding.

- Things have many aspects. It is necessary to have various viewpoints.
- Described information is only an expression from one perspective.
- Acquiring established information seems tedious.

▼ Therefore

Collect a lot of information on what you wish to learn about, and understand it from various angles.

Acquire a lot of information from various sources. Integrate the information you collect, and then reconstruct your understanding of the knowledge from many perspectives. When you begin to learn something new, read several introductory books. Even if you cannot understand the content of a book, other books will explain it differently, which will help your understanding. Moreover, you will find what is referenced many times in several books and recognize it as general opinion. On the other hand, differing content among sources highlights original opinion.

No.13

Skill Embodiment

Continue practicing until you acquire the desired skills.

"Practice makes perfect." —— Proverb

You want to acquire a skill, and maybe you've started to learn.

▼ In this context

It is not sufficient to memorize the "how to."

- Learning from experience is easier to remember than mere memorization.
- Skills can be used unconsciously.
- It is difficult to verbalize a skill acquired through experience.
- It is realized by acquiring skills through repetition.

▼ Therefore

Continue practicing a skill repeatedly until it becomes unconscious.

First, try to use a new skill and acquire a sense of it. Then, study the skill and understand it deeply. Finally, practice until you master it. Learning as *Tangible Growth* (15) is a good way to maintain your motivation.

No.14

Language Shower

Submerge yourself in an environment where you are exposed to the language you want to master.

"There is no way to stop sound and have sound." —— Walter J. Ong

You want a good command of a foreign language.

▼ In this context

Mastering languages is difficult.

- The sense of a language is affected by the nature and culture where it is used.
- Expressions enable you to convey what you want to say.
- It takes a long time to master a language.

▼ Therefore

Establish an environment where you can always listen to and read a foreign language.

If you want to master a foreign language, establish your environment — for example using mobile media — to continue listening to and reading it. Then, make rules to use the language every day, for example, listen to an online radio broadcast or audio book in the background. Physically recording your learning activities as *Tangible Growth* (15) is a good way to maintain your motivation.

No.15

Tangible Growth

You don't grow in a day.

"All of us every single year, we're a different person. I don't think we're the same person all our lives." —— Steven Spielberg

You need to continue practicing for *Skill Embodiment* (13) or taking a *Language Shower* (14).

▼ In this context

It is not easy to keep yourself motivated to learn.

- It takes a long time before you realize the effect of learning.
- It is difficult to maintain your motivation to work hard.

▼ Therefore

Record your learning activities so you can reflect on your path and improve.

Underline passages and write notes when reading books, set out the books and papers you've read, or hang your own work on the wall. Sometimes, look back at your learning path to realize how your knowledge and skills have grown.

Patterns for Creation

Nos. 16 - 27

16 Thinking in Action
17 Prototyping
18 Field Diving

19 A Bug's-Eye & Bird's-Eye View
20 Hidden Connections
21 Triangular Dig

22 Passion for Exploration
23 Brain Switch
24 Fruit Farming

25 Attractive Expressions
26 The First-Draft-Halfway-Point
27 Acceleration to the Next

No.16

Thinking in Action

Creating prototypes or diving into fields
deepens your thinking.

"The way to get started is to quit talking and begin doing." —— Walt Disney

"The only source of knowledge is experience." —— Albert Einstein

You have been studying by reading books, articles, and other written material.

▼ In this context

It is difficult to get out of a situation when stuck.

- It is not easy to change your understanding without interacting with your environment.
- It is difficult to foresee all possible challenges before carrying out your plan.
- Creation and practice make you aware of your limitations.

▼ Therefore

Deepen your thought process by creating prototypes and doing fieldwork.

Create prototypes through *Prototyping* (17) to improve your ideas and gain new insight. Acquire knowledge through fieldwork and *Field Diving* (18), and the knowledge gained will give you a deeper insight.

No.17

Prototyping

It is not until you create prototypes
that you figure out what you really want to make.

"My hand is the extension of the thinking process —— the creative process."
—— Tadao Ando

"A picture is worth a thousand words. a good prototype is worth a thousand pictures." —— Tom Kelly

"Without craftsmanship, inspiration is a mere reed shaken in the wind"
—— Johannes Brahms

You have an idea and are almost ready to implement it.

▼ In this context

You cannot clarify an image of what you will create.

- It is not until you take steps to achieve the objective that you find it clear.
- Making things opens possibilities to enter your next stage of learning.
- It is difficult to discuss an idea without a concrete image of it.

▼ Therefore

Create prototypes and consider how to improve them.

Create a prototype and find out what doesn't work. Consider other approaches to your problems and re-create the prototype. Using the prototypes, share your ideas with others and create better prototypes than before.

No.18

Field Diving

It is not until diving into the field
that you touch upon reality.

"A desk is a dangerous place from which to watch the world."
—— John Le Carré

"Experience without theory is blind, but theory without experience is mere intellectual play. " —— Immanuel Kant

"The map is not the territory" —— Alfred Korzybski

You are thinking about and interested in an actual problem.

▼ In this context

You cannot touch upon reality only by referring to documents.

- A description of a subject is not the subject itself.
- In the field, knowledge exists on the spot.
- Some things are certain or clear to some people, but not to the others.
- The deeper you are in the field, the more you lose objectivity because you are inevitably affected.

▼ Therefore

Dive into the field and work with the people actually concerned while maintaining an outsider's viewpoint.

Search for a field that you are interested in. Dive into the field, and observe what is going on. Understand the context and intention of the activities while interacting with the people concerned. Deepen your understanding of reality by reconsidering your experiences from a certain perspective.

No.19

A Bug's-Eye & Bird's-Eye View

Alternate between two points of view:
look at the whole, then look at the details.

"The eye altering, alters all." —— William Blake

You are studying what you want to understand or working on creating an output.

▼ In this context

You have trouble improving the quality of an idea or mediocre result.

- What is seen depends on the viewpoint.
- It is difficult to view the whole while focusing on details.
- It is difficult to focus on details while looking at the whole.
- It is difficult to have two viewpoints simultaneously.

▼ Therefore

Alternate between viewing the whole and details.

Be aware of the details when working on something from a whole viewpoint (bird's-eye view). For example, if you've thought of the whole, create a specific image of the content. Then, be aware of the whole when working on something from a detailed viewpoint (bug's-eye view). For example, if you've searched for an appropriate expression in your paper, confirm the context. Change the viewpoint and repeat the process several times or as many times as you can.

No.20

Hidden Connections

An unexpected connection is exciting.

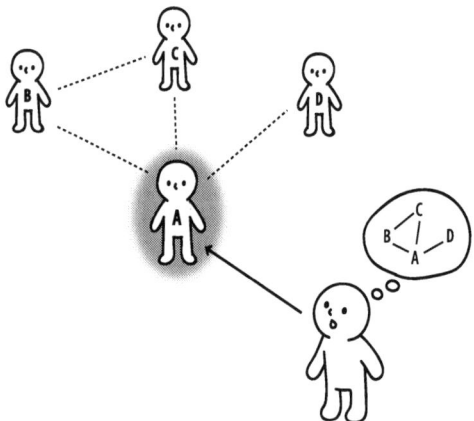

"We build too many walls and not enough bridges." —— Isaac Newton

"Creativity involves breaking out of established patterns in order to look at things in a different way." —— Edward de Bono

"The most exciting attractions are between two opposites that never meet." —— Andy Warhol

You are studying something from a typical viewpoint.

▼ In this context

Unexpected discoveries hardly manifest from conventional classifications.

- It looks good if it is what you are already accustomed to.
- It is necessary to find new meanings of connections between things when you apply a new viewpoint.
- Increasing the number of elements makes if difficult to grasp the whole because the connections between them are drastically increased.

▼ Therefore

Explore hidden connections between things for inspiration.

Find hidden connections between different fields that share the same terms. Think about how and why these things are connected, and make a new category for each connection. Then, consider other things that can be connected to the new category.

No.21

Triangular Dig

Broaden the hole if you want to dig deeper.

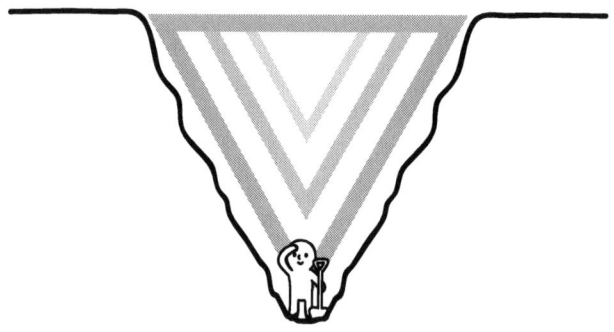

"There is no blue without yellow and without orange."—— Vincent Van Gogh

You're interested in something, but you have only a shallow understanding of it.

▼ In this context

It is difficult to develop your understanding of what you almost know.

- Knowledge does not exist alone but is embedded in the web of knowledge.
- Knowledge comprises various abstract levels.
- Not all related knowledge falls in the same category.

▼ Therefore

Acquire knowledge indirectly related to what you want to understand, and you will understand it better.

First, acquire knowledge in the same category of what you want to learn, and you will understand its features. For example, if you learn Java language, gain knowledge on other programming languages (e.g., C language). This will help you better understand the features of Java. Then, acquire knowledge related to what you want to learn and reconsider its meaning in relationship to this knowledge. For example, if you learn Java, gain knowledge on algorithms and data structures, design patterns, and computer architecture. Then, you will understand the background of Java and the meaning of that language in each relationship to the acquired knowledge.

No.22

Passion for Exploration

It is difficult to carry out hard explorations without passion.

"The only way to do great work is to love what you do." —— Steve Jobs

"Pilots take no special joy in walking. Pilots like flying." —— Neil Armstrong

After acquiring knowledge and improving skills, you finally need to choose the subject you will now explore.

▼ In this context

It is difficult to choose a subject to explore.

- There are many subjects in many fields.
- You never know untill you try.
- It is difficult to continue working hard for something you are not required to do.

▼ Therefore

Choose a topic that you can be passionate about — something that you can "love" or are "passionate" about.

Consider what issues you are interested in or aware of. Your interest is what you love, and your awareness of issues is what you are angry about. Find a field related to your interest or awareness of the issues. Also, make your topic more concrete in the field. Reconsider your topic according to social needs and academic contributions.

No.23

Brain Switch

Both logic and intuition are necessary
for creative thinking.

"Logic will get you from A to B. Imagination will take you everywhere."
—— Albert Einstein

"True creativity often starts where language ends." —— Arthur Koestler

You are creating an output, and you've made some progress.

▼ In this context

Logical thinking is not sufficient to achieve a breakthrough without intuitive thinking and vice versa.

- Logical thinking promotes acute analysis, inference, and persuasion.
- Intuitive thinking inspires good ideas, expressions, and impression.
- It is difficult to be logical and intuitive simultaneously.

▼ Therefore

Switch between the two modes of logical and intuitive thinking.

If you begin to think logically, deliberate as logically as possible. If you begin to think intuitively, exercise imagination as intuitively as possible. Switch thinking modes when you reach a dead end. If you have thought logically, modify to more attractive expressions. For example, when you are writing, draw pictures of what you want to express in words. In contrast, if you have thought intuitively, modify to achieve greater coherence. For example, when you come up with a new idea, think of the logic behind it. By switching thinking modes, you can find new perspectives.

No.24

Fruit Farming

Start small, nurture growth,
and your activity will bear fruit!

"The entire fruit is already present in the seed." —— Tertullian

"Nothing great is created suddenly, any more than a bunch of grapes or a fig. If you tell me that you desire a fig. I answer you that there must be time. Let it first blossom, then bear fruit, then ripen." —— Epictetus

You are planning to create an output, but your vision might be too big.

▼ In this context

It is difficult to produce a big result at once.

- It takes a long time to produce ripe fruit.
- It is difficult to keep working on a task when your efforts seem ineffective.
- A concrete result allows you to move forward with the next plan.

▼ Therefore

Do your best to shape your idea, and then nurture it.

Clarify what you want to do. To achieve steps, nurture your idea and develop concrete results. At this stage, your fruit will still be small. Then, show your results to others. If some colleagues are interested in your activity, invite them to join you. Continue nurturing your ideas until your results bear fruit!

No.25

Attractive Expressions

The way of expression is the message.

"The medium is the message." —— Marchall McLuhan

"If you just communicate you can get by. But if you skillfully communicate, you can work miracles." —— Jim Rohn

"So emotions play an important communicative role." —— Donald Norman

You are starting to develop your presentation to share your idea or product with others.

▼ In this context

Your idea/product seems to be unattractive to others.

- It is impossible to express an idea attractively without understanding why your idea is attractive.
- Each person's evaluation criteria and preferences are different.

▼ Therefore

Find better ways of expression to attract others.

Think about what makes your idea attractive, and use expressions that others can easily understand. Change your way of expression flexibly according to other's reactions. Continually improve your approach to expressing ideas whenever you give a presentation. See also ***Presentation Patterns***, another volume of this catalogue series, about patterns to achieve Creative Presentations.

No.26

The First-Draft-Halfway-Point

Prepare an initial draft to clarify your understanding,
and then re-write it again and again for readers.

"Words do not express thoughts very well. They always become a little different immediately after they are expressed, a little distorted, a little foolish." —— Hermann Hesse

"The more the marbles wastes, the more the statue grows."
—— Michelangelo

You are writing your ideas to share them with others.

▼ In this context

The initial draft is not suitable to be read by others.

- Writing helps organize and deepen your thoughts.
- Writing tends to reflect the thinking process.
- It is not until your paper is written that you can grasp the whole.

▼ Therefore

After finishing an initial draft, improve it objectively, considering whether readers will easily understand.

Thoroughly check if it is clear, concise, and structured logically. Furthermore, considering both sentence and chapter structure will help you alter content more precisely. Occasionally, don't hesitate to discard sections if they are inappropriate. Thereafter, read it from the beginning and determine if readers will understand it. The level of description and definition of terms depends on your target audience. Then, ask others to read it, and get as much feedback as possible. Finally, listen to the rhythm of words, flow of sounds, and check for correct punctuation. By reading aloud, you can more easily recognize errors and inconsistencies. Also, proofread many times for typographical errors.

No.27

Acceleration to the Next

Just before achieving your current goal,
set the next one and hit the accelerator again.

"Intelligence without ambition is a bird without wings." —— Salvador Dalí

You have almost achieved your goal.

▼ In this context

Your motivation is faltering even though the goal is within reach.

- Just before achieving the goal, motivation tends to decrease.
- The process of finally finishing work is always difficult.
- Pursuing the goal forces you into more energetic activities.

▼ Therefore

Set and accelerate toward the next goal to pass through the current goal without slowing down.

Think of the meaning of your activity, and imagine what you should do after achieving your immediate goal. Then, set the next goal and consider the current goal as a milestone along the way. An image of the bigger goal drives you closer to finishing your work.

Patterns for Openness

Nos. 28 - 39

28 Community of Learning
29 Serendipitous Encounters
30 Good Rivals

31 Talking Thinker
32 Leaning by Teaching
33 Firm Determinations

34 Questioning Mind
35 The Right Way
36 Brave Changes

37 Frontier Finder
38 Self-Producer
39 Be Extreme!

No.28

Community of Learning

Two heads or more are likely better than one.

"A person who can create ideas worthy of note is a person who has learned much from others." —— Konosuke Matsushita

You've realized that what you are starting to work on is a challenging problem or activity.

▼ In this context

What you want to study is too big and too difficult to explore alone.

- A person's time is limited.
- A person's knowledge is limited.
- Knowing various viewpoints leads to a deeper understanding.
- It is difficult to continue efforts alone.

▼ Therefore

Build a community of learning with people who share similar interests.

Form a plan to build a "community of learning," thinking about what type of workshops or projects you want to conduct. Recruit members from your surroundings who are interested in your plan. Then, decide how to demonstrate your efforts. For example, write a paper, publish online, or conduct a seminar; these will sustain your activities. Based on this plan, recruit more members beyond your acquaintances with similar interests. Thereafter, hold frequent formal and informal meetings. Sometimes, reflect on what you have done to maintain member motivation.

No.29

Serendipitous Encounters

You can find someone sharing your interest
where you are interested in.

"I don't believe in accidents. There are only encounters in history. There are no accidents." —— Pablo Picasso

You want peers/colleagues to share and discuss topics related to your interest.

▼ In this context

There are few opportunities to meet people with similar interests as you.

- It is not until you go into the field that you start to make new opportunities.
- It is difficult to know others' interests without any event.

▼ Therefore

Find people sharing your interests by getting involved in the field you are interested in.

Join a project related to your interests, and meet people with similar interests.; visit exhibitions related to your area of interest. Probably, the people at the exhibition have similar interests; or read books referenced in your favorite books or in books written by co-authors of your favorite author.

No.30

Good Rivals

Find good rivals, and inspire each other.

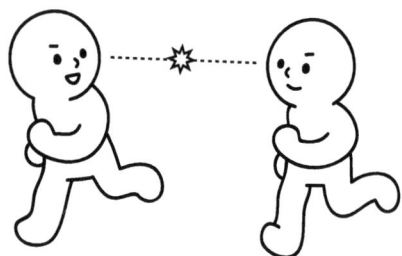

"If you have no critics you'll likely have no success." —— Malcolm S. Forbes

"The best way to cheer yourself up is to try to cheer somebody else up." —— Mark Twain

You've realized that you need to spend considerable time on achieving your goal.

▼ In this context

It is difficult to maintain efforts alone.

- Motivation decreases if others don't recognize your effort.
- A person who does his best touches other's hearts.
- It is difficult to keep working on a task when your attempts seem futile.

▼ Therefore

Make good rivals and inspire each other.

Find people who do their best or to whom you do not want to "lose" to. It doesn't matter what the theme or field is. Then, consider how you will encourage your rival when your rival encourages you. Motivate yourself by competing with your rival. Share results with each other to share progress.

No.31

Talking Thinker

Talk about your idea,
don't be a silent "thinking reed."

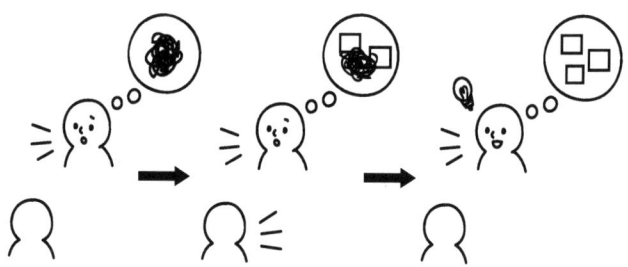

"Man is but a reed, the most feeble thing in nature, but he is a thinking reed." —— Blaise Pascal

"Early and frequent releases are a critical part of the Linux development model. Linus was treating his users as co-developers in the most effective possible way: Release Early. Release Often. And Listen to your customers." —— Eric S. Raymond

You've worked on developing your idea, but it is unclear.

▼ In this context

Thinking alone often brings you to a dead end.

- It is difficult to explain what you do not really understand.
- It is difficult to understand an explanation that is not logically organized.
- It is difficult to realize your own lack of understanding by yourself.

▼ Therefore

Explain what you think verbally to improve your idea.

Find partners who will listen to your idea, and explain what you think rephrase sections that partners do not understand clearly and explain the sections they find most interesting in detail. Improve your method of explanation by reflecting on your oratory skills. Then, find your next audience and explain using your newly improved method.

No.32

Learning by Teaching

You can learn many things by teaching
as well as being taught.

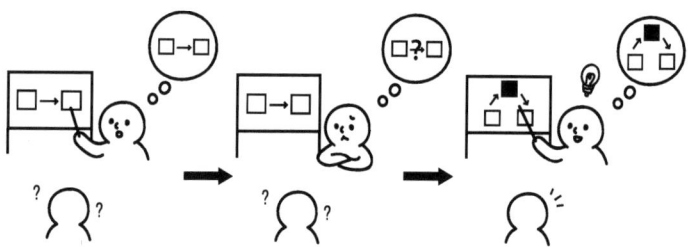

"You teach best what you most need to learn." —— Richard Bach

"Teaching is the highest form of understanding." —— Aristotle

"Making the simple complicated is commonplace. Making the complicated simple —— awesomely simple —— that's creativity."
—— Charles Mingus

You've studied a certain topic to some extent so far.

▼ In this context

You have no idea how to improve your understanding.

- It is difficult to find misunderstanding in what you assume to be understood.
- It is difficult to understand an explanation that is not logically organized.

▼ Therefore

Teach others your knowledge while considering their levels, and you can gain understanding on various levels.

Share your knowledge. For example, it is good to help a subordinate's on a project. Also, it is a good idea to become a Teaching Assistant. Consider how to teach and share your knowledge according to your audience's level. Then, develop a teaching method, comparing several ways of explaining or giving examples of introductions. Then, improve your knowledge and skills if necessary. As you acquire more knowledge and skills, your explanations will become clearer. Teach people according to their abilities and needs, and modify your approach to explaining ideas by observing their responses.

No.33

Firm Determination

Shape up your determination.
Restricting determination to your mind is not sufficient.

"Our power is in our ability to decide." —— Buckminster Fuller

"No! Try not. Do, or do not. There is no try." —— Yoda, in "Star Wars"

You are facing a challenge.

▼ In this context

It is too easy to give up on challenging activities.

- It takes a long time to accomplish something related to your activity or to acquire skills.
- It is impossible to do many things simultaneously.

▼ Therefore

Firmly determine what you are going to do, and establish the environment needed to concentrate on it.

Set your goal concretely, and visualize your success. Then, schedule sufficient time for the activity. Publicly declare your determination to avoid an easy retreat.

No.34

Questioning Mind

Never forget to ask "why?"

"A great many people think they are thinking when they are merely rearranging their prejudices." —— William James

"To doubt everything or to believe everything are two equally convenient solutions; both dispense with the necessity of reflection." —— Henri Poincaré

"It requires strength and courage to swim against the stream, while any dead fish can float with it." —— Samuel Smiles

You've dedicated yourself to a certain activity.

▼ In this context

You cannot find any obvious reasons for what you are doing.

- People frequently accept the trends and opinions of dominant groups for no reason.
- It is difficult to think of activities that you are involved with.
- Things you are used to are always reassuring.

▼ Therefore

Confirm the meanings of your assumptions by questioning yourself again.

Reflect on what you have done so far, and ask yourself why you did it such a manner. Then, examine your activities to check whether they suit your interests. If you find a gap between your interests and activities, change your activities to conform to your interests. Redefine or completely give up your activities if they lack appropriate meaning.

No.35

The Right Way

Is your current approach
really leading you to your goal?

"There's a way to do it better —— find it." —— Thomas A. Edison

"You cannot change your destination overnight, but you can change your direction overnight." —— Jim Rohn

"Seek not to follow in the footsteps of men of old; seek what they sought."
—— Basho Matsuo

You are working on your activity in a certain way.

▼ In this context

The wrong way will lead you away from your goal.

- There is more than one way to achieve an objective.
- A certain path to success is uncertain.
- Things you are accustomed to tend to be more reassuring.

▼ Therefore

Consider whether your current way is actually correct; then quickly change your approach as necessary.

Verify whether your approach to achieve goals related to your research is correct. Then, think about other methods if your current approach is inappropriate. Look at other fields to seek out other approaches. For example, you can solve sustainable development problems through product design or you can solve software development problems through pattern language. Change your approach if you find a better one. Reconsider your goal if you cannot find the right approach.

No.36

Brave Changes

Discarding what you have
is a beginning to exploring new possibilities.

"Courage is resistance to fear, mastery of fear —— not absence of fear."
—— Mark Twain

"Intelligence is the ability to adapt to change. " —— Stephen Hawking

"Change before you have to." —— Jack Welch

You've just realized there is no clear purpose to your activity or that your current approach is inappropriate.

▼ In this context

There seems to be no solution to the current dilemma.

- Things you are accustomed to tend to be more reassuring.
- Giving up a present activity you have steadfastly worked on creates anxiety.
- Inexperience is needed to broaden your perspective.

▼ Therefore

Discard previous themes and approaches to achieve a wider view for the future.

Look back at what you dealt with. Then, understand what you have and have not done. Consider whether such a suspension causes problems when you give up. Prepare to restart before you really give up. For example, keep all related files in a specific location or bind research materials into one file. Forget everything you have done and reconsider what you want to do. It is important to ignore your suspended work. When you find what you want to do, just work on it. You can resume suspended work at anytime and you can apply what you have learned toward the new study.

No.37

Frontier Finder

You cannot venture on a new journey
without knowing where the frontiers are.

"If I have seen further than others, it is by standing upon the shoulders of giants." —— Isaac Newton

"In rivers, the water that you touch is the last of what has passed and the first of that which comes; so with present time." —— Leonardo da Vinci

You've begun your exploration.

▼ In this context

You have to know the frontiers of exploration to conduct valuable activities.

- Academic research, art, and business are activities to explore new fields yet to be mastered.
- Basic knowledge is required to understand what is discussed at the frontier.
- These frontiers expand every day.

▼ Therefore

Grasp the frontier of the field, and then acquire the knowledge needed to reach it.

Know the frontier by reading journals or attending conferences related to your field. In addition, acquire the knowledge needed to understand activities at the frontier. It is useful and exciting to read introductory material and view a documentary on current, leading-edge research because you will become aware of various trials and errors at the frontier. Them, design your research plan and carry it out. Keep following and try to close in on the advancing frontier.

No.38

Self-Producer

Become your own producer.

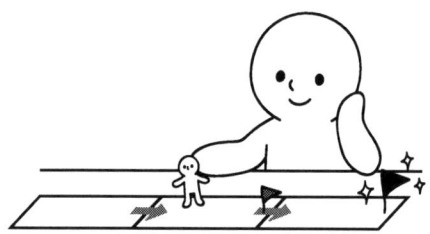

"Life isn't about finding yourself. Life is about creating yourself."
—— George Bernard Shaw

"You have to learn the rules of the game. And then you have to play better than anyone else." —— Albert Einstein

"The best way to predict the future is to invent it." —— Alan Kay

Your goal is clear, and you have started to engage in your activity.

▼ In this context

It is difficult to design your career despite your attempts.

- Every person is constrained by time.
- Your approaches and activities change with your viewpoints.
- It is impossible to describe something persuasively and attractively if you do not thoroughly understand it.

▼ Therefore

Design a concrete plan to achieve your goal while inventing your future.

Clarify your objectives and the means to attain them. Then, Set up short-term and long-term goals and design a process to attain them. For example, imagine what you want to be after a year and set up milestones to achieve your goals. Thereafter, plan specific procedures to reach designated goals. Summarize activities to achieve your objectives and talk to other people about them.

No.39

Be Extreme!

The distinguished were often (regarded as) extreme.

"Whenever you find yourself on the side of the majority, it is time to pause and reflect." —— Mark Twain

"In order to be irreplaceable one must always be different." —— Coco Chanel

"Do not go where the path may lead, go instead where there is no path and leave a trail." —— Ralph Waldo Emerson

Your dedication to activities has established your reputation. You, however, feel it is not sufficient.

▼ In this context

Despite your best efforts, you and your results hardly see the light of day.

- Slight differences are hardly noticed.
- There are no criteria to evaluate the truly new.
- Good things tend to get better.

▼ Therefore

Think strategically on where you can/want to be distinguished from others.

Imagine a vision where you are distinguished and reaping the successes of the distinguished in other fields. Then, understand the strategy needed to reach that vision, and follow in the footsteps of others who are equally distinguished. Devote yourself to studying hard and exploring exhaustively.

How To Use

How To Use Learning Patterns

Learning Patterns have several uses, which can be implemented alone or n a group, as follows.

1. Diagnosing Yourself

You can diagnose yourself on the basis of grouping patterns according to whether or not you has prior experience with each pattern. Reading through the patterns, categorize them into two groups, "Have Experience With" and "Have No Experience With," and write down the results. If you are unsure of a pattern's exact meaning, or if you have not tried the pattern before, then categorize it into the "Have No Experience With" group. When you have grouped all of the patterns, you should be able to develop an overview of your learning experience.

2. Drawing Future Visions

You can use also Learning Patterns to develop your plan of learning. This, too, can be performed either alone or as a team. Read the pattern pages in this book; then, choose and write down patterns that you want to actualize in the near future. If you are doing this as a team, discuss each pattern before writing it down. After the categorization is complete, examine the selected patterns and discuss how they can be actualized.

3. Improving Your Learning

Learning Patterns can be used to improve your way of learning. Examine the 40 patterns (if in a team, discuss them) to categorize them into the three groups: "Practicing," "Want to Practice," and "Not Practicing." The patterns you want to improve will go into the "Want to Practice" group while the patterns that you choose not to use at present will go into the "Not Practicing" group. After the categorization is complete, examine each pattern placed in the "Want to Practice" group and discuss how the pattern can be actualized.

4. Reflecting on Your Learning

At the end of the school term or after a project is completed, the Learning Patterns can be used to reflect on your learning. Categorize the 40 patterns into one of the three groups: "Practicing," "Partially Practicing," and "Not Practicing." If you or your team feels that you have successfully accomplished what the pattern says, then it goes into the ""Practicing" or "Partially Practicing" group as appropriate. If not, then place it in the "Not Practicing" group. The next step is to think about or discuss the positive effects that applying patterns had on your learning. Then, think about and discuss how the unpracticed patterns could serve as a basis for future improvements.

5. Case Studies

You can use the Learning Patterns as tools for case studies of creative learning. Review stories about learning obtained from books or from interviews of people. Examine the 40 patterns (if in a team, discuss) to categorize them into three groups: "Practicing," "Partially Practicing," and "Not Practicing." Use the patterns grouped in the "Practicing" or the "Partially Practicing" groups to think about and discuss why the learning was effective.

6. Dialogues

Learning Patterns enable people to share past experiences of creative learning. This activity should be done in a group. Choose a pattern (or patterns) and share the story with the group.

7. Interviews

You can interview others to hear stories about the patterns you want to use in the future. This activity should be done in a group. Choose a pattern (or patterns) about which you want to hear stories. If any person in the group has a story about the pattern, then that person should share it. You can also choose a pattern that you have already experienced but for which you want to hear additional stories.

Learning Pattern Cards

If you get the card type used in the Learning Patterns, it is easy to manipulate and think about the patterns in the table. The deck consists of three types of cards: Pattern Cards, Activity Cards, and Instruction Cards.

Each of the 40 Pattern Cards describes one of the Learning Patterns. The face of a Pattern Card contains the Pattern Name, a One-liner, an Illustration, and the pattern's Solution. The back of the Pattern Card contains the Context and Problem along with the Pattern Number and Category to which the pattern belongs.

The Activity Cards are for use in workshops. Detailed descriptions can be found in the "Card Uses" printed on the Instruction Cards. The Instruction Cards describe how to use the cards.

Learning Pattern Cards are provided by CreativeShift Lab, and you can buy the cards from Amazon.com (www.amazon.com).

Pattern Card

 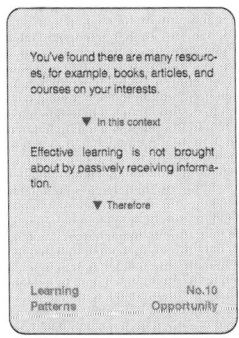

107

Activity Card

Instruction Card

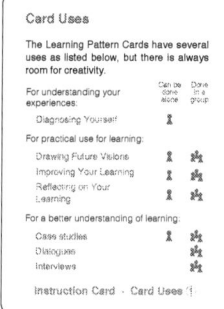

Pattern Dialogue Workshop

You can hold Pattern Dialogue Workshops using the Learning Patterns shown below. The workshop provides an opportunity for the participants to reflect upon their experiences and to improve the sense of learning using the Learning Patterns.

In this workshop, first, ask participants to recall their learning experiences in terms of the provided Learning Patterns. You also ask them to choose patterns they wish to master in the near future. Then, participants are free to mingle and to find and talk with other participants. When they find someone who has experienced one of the patterns they want to master, they listen to the other participant's story.

The workshop provides a clear demonstration of how pattern languages can be used as media for people to talk about their experiences, even if such pattern languages are from domains where people do not often discuss their experiences. This usage of pattern language as a medium for narratives suggests a new possibility for introducing pattern languages into your community.

Pattern Dialogue Workshops with Learning Patterns have been held at the Faculty of Policy Management and Faculty of Environment and Information Studies, Keio University, since 2011. Almost all freshmen at the two faculties—900 students a year—have participated in the workshop, where they talk about their experiences in light of the patterns. Pattern Dialogue Workshops have also been held at several international conferences.

In all these workshops, we always observed the ability of pattern languages to encourage participants to talk about experiences that they seldom mention in their daily life. The following are the feedbacks from the students.

"The workshop helped me remember these past episodes—and more importantly—how much I could already do."

"At first I felt shy and didn't want to talk as much, but soon it became fun searching for people with patterns and talking to them."

"I think the workshop gives its participants a good experience; in that, it gives us an opportunity to ask questions for our own growth, and then, answer questions of others with our own experiences. Such an opportunity is hard to achieve in our daily conversations—especially with so many people."

Creation Process of Learning Patterns

Learning Patterns were created by the following process, which I call the "Holistic Mining" process. The project, led by Takashi Iba, was a collaborative work with 8 students at Iba Laboratory, Keio University.

The original pattern ideas were mined from the project members' own experiences. Through having members with a variety of experience regarding learning, ideas for understanding a "good" learning were elicited through brainstorming. At this point of the project, we did not define the term *Creative Learning*, since definitions would restrict the flow of ideas.

In the brainstorming process, members jot down attributes they think are important for active learning. Each idea is given its own post-it note; the originator talks about it briefly, then sticks the note onto the table. Members gave specific episodes from their prior experience when offering ideas so everyone knew the significance of each note on the table. The goal of this procedure is to glean as many ideas as possible for potential patterns. Repetitions, add-ons, opposite opinions, anything and everything was welcome. Selection and grouping were postponed till later. As a result of the brainstorming session, 300 potential ideas for patterns were collected.

These ideas were organized using the KJ method. The KJ method was proposed by Jiro Kawakita (hence the name) for converging ideas emerging during the brainstorming phase. In the KJ method, ideas that are thought to have similar attributes are grouped together and placed close to each another. However, these similarities must not be mere superficial resemblances, core traits and functions must be observed and talked through before a single connection between two notes can be made. Another important aspect to keep in mind is that notes must be moved in terms of pairs.

Once the process starts, clusters of notes having similar ideas start to appear. It becomes tempting to connect an idea to a group of ideas, but this again would be superficial. Categories of ideas will emerge as a result of connecting ideas by pairs. When members think that all ideas have been mapped into the correct relations, the KJ method is finished. By this time, the notes would have formed emergent clusters, each of which is a potential pattern. Some contained dozens of notes, while others contained only one note. The 300 ideas from the brainstorming phase converged to 50 clusters.

Then, after deep talks, similar cluster were integrated. This process reduced the number of clusters to 40, close to the final number of patterns in the published version. Also at this stage, the structure of the Learning Patterns had been roughly defined.

Members then split into two groups: a writing team and an illustration team. Writing team members allocated the 40 patterns between them and wrote the patterns on the basis of the labels as homework. During lab sessions, the writing team would go over each pattern together, one at a time, offering comments on how the expressions could be improved. Once this was complete, a different person would rewrite the pattern. This process was repeated several times, meaning that each pattern went through five to seven rounds of revisions, each with a different author.

During this final stage, some changes to the structure of the pattern language were made. As the details on the patterns were further delineated, members further understood what they are truly saying. The structure of the Learning Patterns shown in the paper is a final version, and it has been achieved after it underwent many changes on the way to completion.

The illustration team went through a similar process. The team would first read through the pattern and suggest images for potential illustrations. Relevant metaphors proved helpful to inspire an image. Members would then each draw an illustration for the same pattern. They would offer comments on each other's ideas and thus work towards the final version of the illustration.

The words and illustrations of a pattern are deeply entwined. One affects the other, and cannot be thought of in isolation. At lab sessions, writing team members would make comments on the illustration, and the illustration team would collaborate on phrases or pattern names. This mutual interdependence created a pattern language with deeply interlocked parts.

Thus we finally constructed a pattern language for *Creative Learning* consisting of 40 patterns.

References

Alexander, C. (1979) *The Timeless Way of Building*, Oxford University Press, New York.

Alexander, C., Davis, H., Martinez, J. and Corner, D. (1985) *The Production of Houses*, Oxford University Press, New York.

Alexander, C., Ishikawa, S., Silverstein, M., Jacobson, M., Fiksdahl-King, I. and Angel, S. (1977) *A Pattern Language: Towns, Buildings, Construction*, Oxford University Press, New York.

Anthony, D.L.G. (1996) 'Patterns for classroom education', in Vlissides, J.M., Coplien, J.O. and Kerth, N.L. (Eds.): *Pattern Languages of Program Design 2*, Addison-Wesley, Boston.

Arao, R., Tamefusa, A., Kadotani, M., Harasawa, K., Sakai, S., Saruwatari, K. and Iba, T. (2012) 'Generative beauty patterns: a pattern language for living lively and beautiful', in *the 19th Conference on Pattern Languages of Programs (PLoP2012)*.

Beck, K. and Cunningham, W. (1987) 'Using pattern languages for object-oriented programs', *OOPSLA-87 Workshop on the Specification and Design for Object-Oriented Programming*.

Bergin, J. (2000) 'Fourteen pedagogical patterns', in *the 15th European Conference on Pattern Languages of Programs (EuroPLoP 2000)*.

Bergin, J., Eckstein, J., Manns, M.L. and Sharp, H. (2011) 'Patterns for active learning', in *the 16th European Conference on Pattern Languages of Programs (EuroPLoP 2011)*.

Furukawazono, T., Seshimo, S., Muramatsu, D. and Iba, T. (2013b) 'Survival language: a pattern language for surviving earthquakes', in *the 20th International Conference on Pattern Language of Programs (PLoP2013)*.

Gabriel, R.P. (1996) *Patterns of Software Tales from the Software Community*, Oxford University Press, New York.

Gamma, E., Helm, R., Johnson, R. and Vlissides, J. (1994) *Design Patterns: Elements of Reusable Object-Oriented Software*, Addison-Wesley, Boston.

Hoover, D. and Oshineye, A. (2009) *Apprenticeship Patterns: Guidance for the Aspiring Software Craftsman*, O'Reilly Media, Sebastopol.

Iba, T. (2011a) 'Pattern Language 3.0 methodological advances in sharing design knowledge', in *the International Conference on Collaborative Innovation Networks 2011 (COINs2011)*.

Iba, T. (2011b) 'Experience mining and dialogues workshop with a pattern language for creative learning', Workshop, in *the International Conference on Collaborative Innovation Networks 2011 (COINs2011)*.

Iba, T. (2011c) 'Experience mining and dialogues workshop with the learning patterns', in *the 2nd Asian Conference on Pattern Languages of Programs (AsianPLoP2011)*.

Iba, T. (2012) 'Pattern Language 3.0: writing pattern languages for human actions', Invited Talk, in *the 19th Conference on Pattern Languages of Programs (PLoP2012)*.

Iba, T. and Isaku, T. (2013) 'Collaboration patterns: a pattern language for creative collaborations', in *the 18th European Conference on Pattern Languages of Programs (EuroPLoP 2013)*.

Iba, T. and Miyake, T. (2010) 'Learning patterns: a pattern language for creative learners II', in *the 1st Asian Conference of Pattern Language of Programs (AsianPLoP2010)*.

Iba, T. and Sakamoto, M. (2011) 'Learning patterns: a pattern language for creative learning', in *the 18th Conference on Pattern Languages of Programs (PLoP2011)*.

Iba, T., Ichikawa, C., Sakamoto, M. and Yamazaki, T. (2011) 'Pedagogical patterns for creative learning', in *the 18th International Conference on Pattern Languages of Programs (PLoP2011)*.

Iba, T., Matsumoto, A. and Harasawa, K. (2012a) 'Presentation patterns: a pattern language for creative presentations', in *the 17th European Conference on Pattern Languages of Programs (EuroPLoP2012)*.

Iba, T., Shimomukai, E., Nakamura, S., Isaku, T. and Tamefusa, A. (2012b) 'Dialogue workshop using the learning patterns', in *the 19th Conference on Pattern Languages of Programs (PLoP2012)*.

Iba, T., Miyake, T., Naruse, M. and Yotsumoto, N. (2009) 'Learning patterns: a pattern language for active learners', in *the 16th Conference on Pattern Languages of Programs (PLoP2009)*.

Köppe, C. (2011) 'Continuous activity: a pedagogical pattern for active learning', in *the 16th European Conference on Pattern Languages of programs (EuroPLoP2011)*.

Manns, M.L. and Rising, L. (2005) *Fearless Change: Patterns for Introducing New Ideas*, Addison-Wesley, Boston.

Matsuzuka, K., Isaku, T., Nishina, S. and Iba, T. (2013) 'Global life patterns: a methodology for designing a personal global life', in *the 4th International Conference on Collaborative Innovation Networks (COINs2013)*.

Nakada, M., Kamada, A. and Iba, T. (2013) 'Personal culture patterns – a pattern language for living with continuous self-fulfillments', in *the 18th European Conference on Pattern Languages of Programs (EuroPLoP2013)*.

Pedagogical Patterns Editorial Board (2012) *Pedagogical Patterns: Advice for Educators*, Createspace, San Bernardino, CA.

Shibuya, T., Seshimo, S., Harashima, Y., Kubota, T. and Iba, T. (2013) 'Educational patterns for generative participant – designing for creative learning', in *the 20th International Conference on Pattern Language of Programs (PLoP2013)*.

Shimomukai, E., Nakamura, S. and Iba, T. (2012) 'Change making patterns: a pattern language for fostering social entrepreneurship', in *the 19th Conference on Pattern Languages of Programs (PLoP2012)*.

Pattern Language 3.0 Catalogue Series

Learning Patterns: A Pattern Language for Creative Learning

Learning Patterns is a set of patterns that describe the secrets of creative learning. It offers 40 patterns, each of which captures an aspect of a good learning. Create opportunities for learning on  your own by launching and implementing your own project, as well as learn by actively creating in collaboration with others!

Presentation Patterns: A Pattern Language for Creative Presentations

Presentation Patterns is a set of patterns that describes the secrets of creative presentations. There are 34 patterns, each of which captures an aspect of a good presentation. Treat your  presentation not as merely a chance to explain your idea, but as a chance for creation. Work with your audience to trigger new findings in them!

Collaboration Patterns: A Pattern Language for Creative Collaborations

Collaboration Patterns is a set of patterns that describes the secrets of creative and collaborative project work. Each of the 34 patterns captures an aspect of a good collaboration.
Create new values that can change the world by collectively producing an emergent synergy that cannot be reduced to any one team member, but can only come from developing the capacity to enhance each other!

All Written by Takashi Iba *with* Iba Laboratory
Published by CreativeShift Lab, 2014

Words for a Journey: The Art of Being with Dementia

Takashi Iba and Makoto Okada (eds.), 2015
Iba Laboratory and Dementia Friendly Japan Initiative

Words for a Journey collects practical knowledge on living with dementia. Though many hold negative impressions of the disease, there are still many who are living well with dementia. This book collects wisdom and stories from such people, and extracts its essence to be shared widely.

Survival Language: A Pattern Language for Surviving Earthquakes

Tomoki Furukawazono and Takashi Iba
with Survival Language Project, 2015

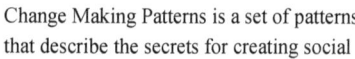

Survival Language is a pattern language to improve survival rates when a catastrophic earthquake occurs. There are twenty patterns, each of which captures practices of Designing for Preparation, Designing for Emergency Action, and Designing for Life After a Quake that form patterns found in the many lessons Japan has learned from numerous earthquakes.

Change Making Patterns: A Pattern Language for Fostering Social Entrepreneurship

Eri Shimomukai and Sumire Nakamura
with Takashi Iba, 2015

Change Making Patterns is a set of patterns that describe the secrets for creating social change. There are 31 patterns, each of which captures the aspects of creatively solving social issues. Launch your own change-making project to tackle social issues in your own context to take part in creating a better world!

Meta-Pattern Language Catalogue Series

Pattern Illustrating Patterns: A Pattern Language for Pattern Illustrating

Takashi Iba
with Iba Laboratory, 2015

Pattern Illustrating Patterns is a set of patterns that describe how and what to draw and what aspects must be considered when creating pattern illustrations. We hope this pattern language will help to include pattern illustration as an approach to visual aid by those considering or creating pattern languages.

Learning Patterns

The Core Patterns

0 Creative Learning

1 Opportunity for Learning
2 Learning by Creating
3 Open Learning

Patterns for Opportunity

4 Jump In
5 Copycat Learner
6 Effective Asking

7 Output-Driven Learning
8 Daily Use of Foreign Language
9 Playful Learning

10 Tornado of Learning
11 Chain of Excitement
12 Quantity brings Quality

13 Skill Embodiment
14 Language Shower
15 Tangible Growth

Patterns for Creation

16 Thinking in Action
17 Prototyping

18 Field Diving

19 A Bug's-Eye & Bird's-Eye View
20 Hidden Connections
21 Triangular Dig

22 Passion for Exploration
23 Brain Switch
24 Fruit Farming

25 Attractive Expressions
26 The First-Draft-Halfway-Point
27 Acceleration to the Next

Patterns for Openness

28 Community of Learning
29 Serendipitous Encounters
30 Good Rivals

31 Talking Thinker
32 Leaning by Teaching
33 Firm Determinations

34 Questioning Mind
35 The Right Way
36 Brave Changes

37 Frontier Finder
38 Self-Producer
39 Be Extreme!

Made in the USA
Columbia, SC
02 August 2019